lots of pots

a girl said, "that man has lots of pots. hē has pots with tops. hē has pots with nō tops."

the man said, "I havₑ lots of cākₑs in pots. I havₑ a pot with a ship in it. I havₑ fish in pots."

the girl said, "can I have a pot fōr

a little fish?"

the man said, "this is a pot fōr a

little fish."

the girl said, "I will tāke this pot

hōme with mē." and shē did.

al and sal

al said, "will wē gō hōme?"

sal said, "nō. wē will gō to that farm."

al said, "will wē have fun on that

farm?"

sal said, "wē can run with a cow.

wē can ēat cōrn. wē can fēēd pigs. wē

can sit in the lāke.”

al said, “I hāte to sit in lākes.”

sō sal and al did not sit in the lāke.

sal and al had fun with the pigs.

a fiꞅh in the rāin

ron met pat in the rāin. ron got wet.

pat got wet.

ron said, "this is not fun."

pat said, "this is fun."

ron said, "I haVₑ wet fēēt. sō I

will gō hōmₑ. I do not nēēd rāin."

pat said, "wē can get fish." →

sō shē got a fish and gāve it to him. →

ron said, "it is fun to get wet if wē →

get fish." →

the pet shop

a girl said to a man, "let us gō to the pet shop." sō the man and the girl went down the rōad.

the man and the girl went in the pet shop. the girl said to the man in the pet shop, "I nēēd a dog."

the man said, "nō. I do not haVe dogs.

I haVe a red cat. let mē get that cat."

sō hē did. and the girl went hōme with

the red cat.

the cow on the rōₐd

lots of men went in a littlₑ car. the

men went down a rōₐd.

a cow sat on the rōₐd. the cow did

not get up. sō the men ran to the cow.

the men said, "wē will lift this cow."

the men did not lift the cow. "this cow

is sō fat wē can not lift it."

the cow said, "I am not sō fat. I can

lift mē." the cow went in the car.

the men said, "now wē can not get

in the car." sō the men sat on the rōad

and the cow went hōme in the car.

a girl and a gōat

a girl was on the rōad to a farm. shē
met a gōat. shē said, "gō with mē to the
farm. wē will pet a pig."

the gōat said, "I pet ducks and I
pet chicks. I do not pet pigs."

the girl said, "it is fun to pet pigs.

pigs ar_e fat."

the gōat said, "I will not gō to the

farm. I will gō to the park and pet

a duck."

sō the gōat went to the park to pet a

duck. and the girl went to the farm to

pet a pig.

pāint that nōse →

a fat dog met a little dog. the fat dog →

had a red nōse. the little dog had a red →

nōse. →

the fat dog said, "I have a red nōse." →

the little dog said, "I wish I did not →

have a red nōse." →

the fat dog got a can of pāint. hē

said, "pāint that nōse."

sō the littlе dog did pāint his nōse. hē

said, "now this nōse is not red."

hē kissеd the fat dog on the ēar. now

the fat dog has pāint on his ēar.

the red hat ➤

the fish had a car and nō hat. shē
said, "I do not nēēd a car. I nēēd a
red hat."

shē met a cow. the cow had a red hat.
the fish said, "can I have that red hat?"
the cow said, "nō."

the fish said, "I will give that cow a

car if she will let me have the hat."

the cow said, "take the hat and give

me a car." so the fish got a red hat

and the cow got a car.

a bug and a dog

a bug and a dog sat on a log. the

dog said, "that bug is sō littlₑ I can not

sēē him on the log."

the bug said, "I am big."

the dog said, "that bug on the log

is not big."

the bug said, "I will ēₐt this log."

and hē did. hē bit and bit and bit at the

log. the bug said, "now that dog can sēē

how big I am."

the dog said, "that bug can ēₐt logs

as well as a big bug can."

the bugs →

a big bug met a little bug. the big bug →

said, "let's gō ēat." sō the big bug āte a →

lēaf and a nut and a rock. the big bug →

said, "that is how big bugs ēat." →

the little bug said, "now I will ēat." →

sō the little bug āte a lēaf and a nut and →

a rock. then the little bug went to a log

and bit the log. she āte the log. then she

āte ten mōre logs.

"wow," the big bug said. "that little

bug can ēat a lot."

the little bug said, "now let's ēat mōre."

the bug bus

a little bug sat on the back of a big dog. "get down," said the dog. "I am not a bus."

the bug did not get down. she went to sleep. the dog said, "I am not a bed."

the dog ran to the pond and went in.

the bug got wet. the bug said, "I am

not a fish. tāke mē back to the sand."

"nō," the dog said.

sō the bug said, "I will get mōre bugs

on this dog." ten bugs cāme and got on

the dog.

the dog said, "I fēēl līke a bug bus."

and the dog went back to the sand with

the bugs.

the man and his bed

a man had a tub. hē said, "I līke to sit in the tub and rub, rub, rub."

then the man said, "now I will slēēp in this bed." but a dog was in his bed.

the dog said, "can I slēēp in this bed?"

the man said, "nō. gō slēēp in the tub."

the dog said, "I līke to slēēp in beds."

the man said, "this dog līkes to slēēp

in beds. sō hē can slēēp with mē. but I

do not līke dogs that bīte."

the dog said, "I do not līke to bīte."

sō the man and the dog went to slēēp.

and the dog did not bīte the man.

the talking cat

the girl was gōīng fōr a walk. shē met a fat cat. "can cats talk?" the girl said.

the cat said, "I can talk. but I do not talk to girls. I talk to dogs."

the girl did not līke that cat. "I do not līke cats that will not talk to mē."

the cat said, "I will not talk to girls."

the girl said, "I do not līke that cat.

and I do not give fish to cats I do not

līke."

the cat said, "I līke fish sō I will

talk to this girl." sō the girl and the cat

āte fish.

the dog that āte fish

a girl went fishing with a dog. that

dog āte fish. the girl did not līke the

dog to ēat fish. "do not ēat the fish," shē

said.

the girl went fishing and the dog went

to slēēp. the girl got fīve fish.

"giv_e mē the fīv_e fish," the dog said.

"nō," the girl said. "mōr_e fish ar_e in the lāk_e. dīv_e in and get them."

sō the dog went in the lāk_e. and the girl went to slēēp.

the end

the rat got a sōrₑ nōsₑ

a rat and a rabbit went down a slīdₑ.

the rabbit went down on his tāil. the

rat said, "I will gō down on the tāil."

the rat went up to the top of the slīdₑ

and slid down on his nōsₑ. hē said, "I

havₑ a sōrₑ nōsₑ."

then hē said, "if a rabbit can gō down

on his tāil, I will do the sāme." hē went

up to the top. but hē cāme down on his

nōse.

the rabbit said, "that rat can not tell

if hē is on his nōse ōr his tāil."

the end

the rich pig

a dog was in the park. it was dark in

the park.

shē ran into a pig. shē said,

"pigs can not gō in this park. pigs livₑ

on farms."

the pig said, "not this pig. I livₑ on a

ship. I am a rich pig."

the dog said, "tāke mē to the ship."

sō the pig did.

but the wāves māde the ship rock.

and the dog got sick.

the end

digging in the yard

a little man had a fat dog. the dog

lived in the yard. the dog dug a hole in

the yard. the little man got mad. "dogs

can not dig in this yard. I will go for a

cop." the dog dug and dug.

the man got a cop. the man said, "that

dog dug a big hōle in the yard."

the cop said, "dogs can not dig in

this yard."

the dog said, "I will stop. can I bē

a cop dog?"

the cop said, "yes. I nēēd a cop dog."

the end

ron said, "yes"

ron's dad tōld him to slēēp in bed.

"yes," ron said. and hē did.

his mom said, "ron, pāint this bed red."

"yes," ron said. hē got the pāint and mād₆ the bed red.

"that is fīne," his mom said.

a big bōy met ron. hē said, "can ron pāint a car red?"

"yes," ron said. and hē māde the car red.

then ron went hōme. his mom said, "ron māde a bed red and a car red. but ron got lots of pāint on ron. ron is red."

sō ron went to the tub and went rub,

rub, rub. now ron is not red.

this is the end.

gōing to the park

a bōy met fīve girls. hē said, "let's gō

to the park."

a girl said, "wē can not sēē the park.

is the park nēar hēre?"

the bōy said, "nō. wē nēēd a car to

get to the park."

the girls said, "wē do not hаvе a car."

the bōy said, "wē can not walk to the

park. and wē can not rīdе to the park.

how will wē get to the park?"

the girls said, "let's run." sō the bōy

and the girls ran to the park.

this is the end.

hunting fōr a dēēr

ann said to her dad, "let's gō fīnd a

dēēr fōr a pet."

sō ann and her dad went hunting fōr

a dēēr. a dēēr cāme up to them. ann

said, "you can bē a pet."

the dēēr said, "nō, a dēēr is not a pet.

dogs ar$_e$ pets. and cats ar$_e$ pets. I am
not a pet. but I will let a girl and her
dad pet mē."

the girl said, "that will bē fun." it was.

now, the girl has a pet dog and a pet
cat. they gō with her to hunt fōr the
dēēr that shē can pet.   the end

a card fōr mother

a bōy sent a card to his mother. the card said, "mother, I love you." but his mother did not get the card.

a cop got the card. shē said, "I am not mother." sō shē gāve the card to her brother.

her brother said, "this card is not

fōr mē. I am not mother."

sō the cop and her brother went to

fīnd mother. they met the bōy.

the bōy said, "you havₑ the card that

I sent to mother. givₑ mē that card."

sō they gāvₑ him the card.

and hē gāv_e the card to his mother.

this is the end.